Boys vs. Girls

Written by
Rob Waring and **Maurice Jamall**

(with contributions by **Julian Thomlinson**)

Before You Read

to scream

to spray

bear

bee

cabin

cage

camp

cow

food

ghost

honey

milk

rat

Ryan

Mike

Faye

Mr. Woods

David

Eric

Gemma

Kerry

"Wow," says John. "This is going to be really fun."
Many students from Bayview High are at Bear Mountain Camp for the weekend. They get off the bus and go to the camp.
"This place looks really great," says John.
"Yes, it does," replies his friend, Faye. "It's my first time here. It's going to be great."
"It looks dirty," says Daniela.
"Don't worry, Daniela," says John. "We'll have a great time."

Everybody is very excited. They want to look at everything. Their teacher, Mr. Harris, says, "This is the boys' cabin. Boys, you're in here." He shows them a small cabin.

"And the girls are in here," says Mrs. Brown. She shows them a different cabin.

"Look at the animals! I love this place," says a boy named David. He shows them some animals next to the boys' cabin. There are lots of animals at the camp.

Bear Mountain Camp Rules

1. Be careful. There are dangers here.

2. Do not walk into the forest alone.

3. Be in your cabins by 8 o'clock and in bed by 9 o'clock.

A little later, a man speaks to everybody. "Okay, everybody. Come here, please. Good morning," he says. "My name's Mr. Woods," he says. "I want you to have a good time when you're here. But there are some camp rules, so please read them."
The students look at the rules. Some of them do not like the rules.
"What? Bed by nine o'clock?" says a boy. His name is Ryan. "No way! Not me!"

np Rules

dangers

forest

3 o'clock
ck.

"Yes. You too," says Mr. Woods. "This place can be dangerous at night. We're near the forest," he says. "There are bears near here. They like to walk around at night."

"Now, let's start with something nice and easy," he says. "How many people know how to milk a cow?" he asks. Nobody says anything.

"Well, now you're going to learn," says Mr. Woods. David says, "Great!" He loves animals. "Oh no!" says Daniela. "I hate milk."

"Okay," says Mr. Woods. "Who can get the most milk? You have 30 minutes. But first I will show you how to do it." Mr. Woods shows them how to milk the cow. "See. It's easy," he says. "Now you try!" The girls and boys start to milk the cows.

"Come on, everybody," says Faye. "We want to win. Let's get a lot of milk."

Gemma is not very interested in milking cows.

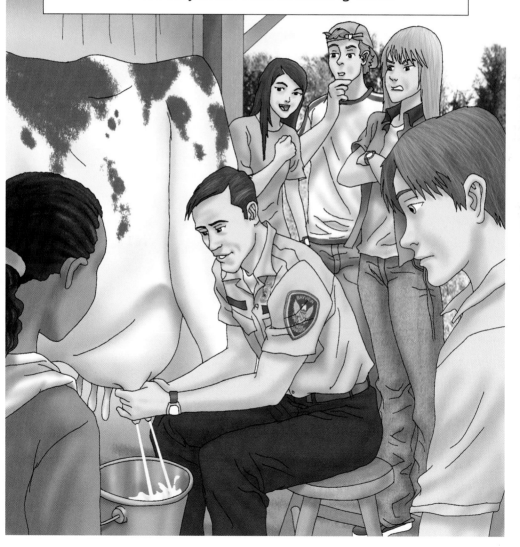

"Come on, Gemma," say Faye and Kerry. "Try! It's fun."
Gemma sits next to the cow and tries to milk it. It is not easy
but she tries hard. But she is not careful. Suddenly, some milk
goes into Ryan's face!

"I'm sorry, Ryan," she says to her brother.

"Hey, be careful!" shouts Ryan angrily. Then Gemma thinks,
"I have an idea."

She smiles. Then she sprays Ryan's friend Eric with the milk!

"Hey, stop that!" says Eric. But the girls all laugh. They are having fun. Then, the other girls spray the boys with milk, too.

"Good job, Kerry. That's a great hit!" says Gemma, laughing. They both spray the boys with more milk. The boys try to spray the girls with milk, too. But they are not very good. Soon, there is milk all over the boys.

"Look at Ryan! He looks like a ghost!" says Kerry.

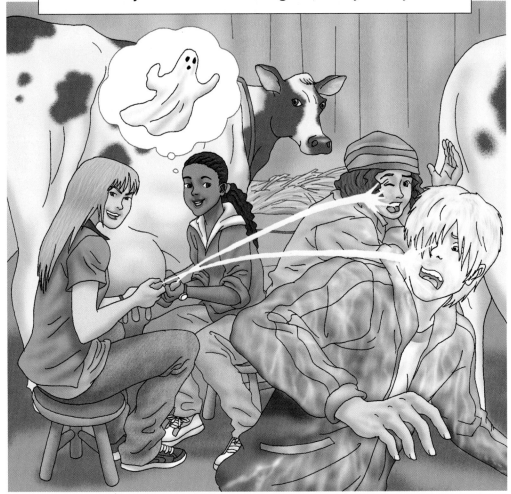

"What's going on here?" shouts Mr. Woods. He looks at the boys.
He says, "You don't know how to milk the cows at all! You're
doing it all wrong. You didn't listen to me."
Eric is angry. "But, Mr. Woods, the girls . . . ," he starts.
Mr. Woods stops him. "I don't want to know!" he says. "You must
stop this. You mustn't spray milk. You should know better!"
"Just wait, Gemma," says Ryan. The boys are angry with the girls.

The boys are walking to their cabin. They are still wet from the milk. "Those girls make me really angry," Eric says. "Let's do something to the girls. What can we do to them? Does anybody have an idea?"

Eric's friend, Mike, says, "Look over there. We can use them." He points to some cages in the camp zoo.

"Use what?" asks Eric. "I don't understand."

"Come with me. I'll show you," says Mike. "I have a plan. This will be great!"

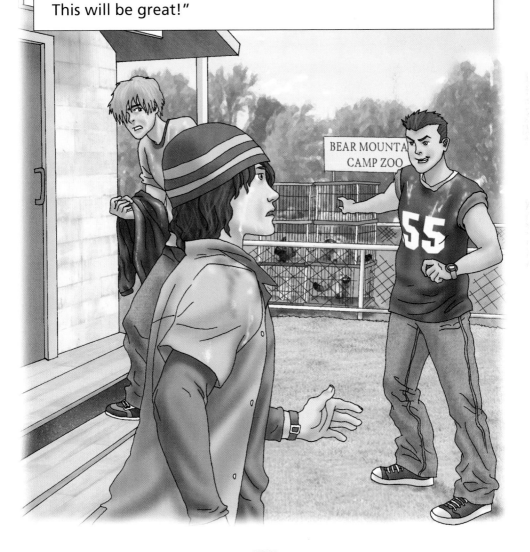

The girls are sitting in their cabin. They are still laughing about the milk.

"They were so wet!" says Gemma.

"And they smelled so bad!" says Faye. They laugh and laugh.

The boys go to the girls' cabin. "This is going to be great!" says Eric.

Ryan pushes the door open. "Hey girls, we have something for you!"

Mike opens the cage and the rats run all over the room. The girls see the rats and start screaming. They jump on the beds. Some girls run for the door.

"Rats! Get out! Get out!" shouts Gemma. The boys laugh. Now the girls are not laughing any more.

"I'm getting out of here," cries Gemma. Faye cannot move. She is scared of rats. The boys laugh and laugh.

"What's going on here?" shouts Mr. Woods. "Who put these rats in here?"

"It wasn't us, Mr. Woods," says Faye. She starts to say, "But the boys . . ."

Mr. Woods stops her. "I don't want to know!" he says. "I don't care who started this. Stop this, right now." He is very angry.

"I want you to enjoy the camp, everybody," he says. "But I don't want any more trouble. Boys, get the rats back into the cage."

"I want you to say sorry to the girls," he says. "You must stop this. Someone will get hurt."

"Sorry, girls," say the boys, but they are still laughing.

The boys are in their cabin. They are talking about the rats. Eric laughs, "They were really frightened. But it was so funny. They screamed and screamed. Did you see Gemma? Ha ha ha!" Just then, somebody comes to the door. Ryan goes to the door and opens it.

"Yes?" says Ryan. "What do you want?"

Faye and Gemma say, "We want to say sorry and we won't do that again."

"Can we come in and talk?" asks Gemma.

"Okay," the boys say. "Come in."

"Are you ready? Here you are, boys," say Faye and Gemma. They spray the boys with cold water. The boys and the cabin are very wet!

"Which do you like more, milk, or water, boys?" laughs Gemma. "Enjoy your drink! Does it feel good?"

"Hey!" says Ryan. "Stop it!"

The girls do not stop. They spray all the boys. They laugh and laugh. The boys are angrier now.

Later that day, Mr. Woods takes them to the camp zoo. The boys look at the rat's cage and they smile.

"This is our small camp zoo," says Mr. Woods. "At this camp, we make milk, and honey."

"Honey? Mr. Woods, did you say you make honey here?" asks David. Mr. Woods asks, "Why? Do you like bees?"

"Sure. Bees are very interesting. We learned about them in school," replies David. "Where do you keep the bees?" he asks.

"We keep our bees over there," says Mr. Woods. He points to some trees.

Later, they go to the camp store. "Here, we sell many things from our camp," Mr. Woods says. "They're very good," he says. "Please buy some."
Mike says quietly, "Hey, Ryan. I have an idea."
"What idea?" asks Ryan. "Tell us."
"First, give me some money," Mike says.
"Money? What do you need money for?" asks Ryan.
"Just give me some money, okay? Then I'll tell you," answers Mike.

They go to the girls' cabin. Mike tells them his idea.
"Bees like honey," says Mike. "So let's put this honey near the girls' cabin, then the bees will come. The girls are frightened of bees."
"Of course! What a great idea!" says Ryan. They put the honey all over the cabin. "Put some on the door, too," he says.
"And here," says Eric. "The bees will go in the window."
"Quick! Let's go. Let's watch from our cabin," says Ryan.

The boys are waiting in their cabin. Ryan hears something. "That's strange. Can you hear something?" asks Ryan.

"Yes," says Mike. "It's coming from over there." He points at the trees. "But it's not bees!"

"Oh no! Bears!" cries Eric. "They're going to the girls' cabin!" David hears them. "Bears? Here?" says David. "Why are they here? What did you do?" he asks.

"We put some honey on the door of the girls' cabin," says Ryan.

"What? Oh no! Don't you know bears like honey?" says David. "Bees *make* honey. They don't *eat* it. Bears do!"

He says, "Eric, run to Mr. Woods and get help. GO!"

The girls hear the noise, too. "What's happening?" asks Gemma. Faye looks out the window.

"Bears! Bears!" she shouts. "Some bears are trying to get into the cabin!"

The bears are everywhere. They go to the doors and the windows.

"The bears want to get in," cries Faye. "Somebody, help us!"

"Help! Help!" shout the girls. "Help us!"

The teachers come to the boys' cabin. They are very surprised to see the bears.

"Oh no! The girls!" says Mrs. Brown. "Help the girls!"

David speaks to everybody. "Okay, everybody. Get all the food you have. Bring it to me now!"

"Excuse me? This is not a time to eat, David," says Mrs. Brown.

"It's for the bears!!" he says. "Do it quickly! Now! Go!"

Everybody runs and gets their food.

David takes their food and runs out of the cabin. "Stay here," he calls.

"No, David!" says Mrs. Brown. She screams. She is very worried about David.

"Don't worry," he says. "They want some food."

David runs to some trees. He puts some food down for the bears. They find the food. They turn to eat it.

"That's it, bears," he says. "Come on." The bears leave the cabins. They go back towards the forest.

Soon, the bears are back in the forest. "Good job, David!" says Mr. Woods.

David is very happy but he says, "It was nothing, really."

Mrs. Brown says to the boys, "Boys, that was very bad of you. You must go and clean the cabin. We want no more trouble."

"Yes, Mrs. Brown," says Mike. "We're very sorry." The boys go to clean the cabin.

"Well, it's good nobody was hurt," says Mrs. Brown. "And good job, David. You did very well!"